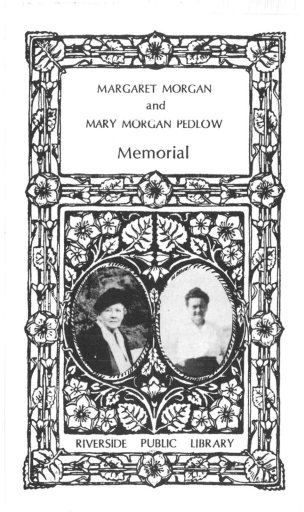

MARGARET MORGAN
and
MARY MORGAN PEDLOW

Memorial

RIVERSIDE PUBLIC LIBRARY

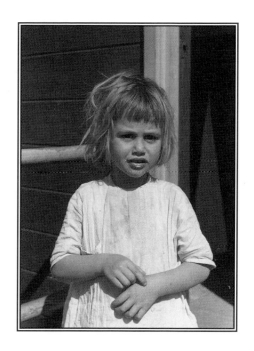

Children
of the
DUST DAYS

Children
of the
DUST DAYS

Karen Mueller Coombs

Carolrhoda Books, Inc./Minneapolis

For Ellen, my friend since fourth grade, who weathered the wind and the dust with me and helped sing "Calendar Girl" under the caragana hedge

Page one: During the dust days, this girl's family had no farm of their own. They traveled from place to place in search of work.
Page two: Farm children in Idaho, 1936
Opposite page: A boy plays with his dog on a drift of windblown soil in Kansas.

Text copyright © 2000 by Karen Mueller Coombs

Carolrhoda Books, Inc.
A Division of Lerner Publishing Group
241 First Avenue North
Minneapolis, MN 55401 U.S.A.

Website address: www.lernerbooks.com

LIBRARY OF CONGRESS CATALOGING-IN-PUBLICATION DATA

Coombs, Karen Mueller, 1947–
    Children of the dust days / Karen Mueller Coombs.
      p. cm. — (Picture the American past)
    Includes bibliographical references (p.) and index.
    Summary: Focuses on the experiences of children during the Dust Bowl era of the 1930s, when prolonged drought, coupled with farming techniques, caused massive erosion from Texas to Canada's wheat fields.
      ISBN 1-57505-360-8
      1. Dust storms—Great Plains—History—20th century—Juvenile literature. 2. Great Plains—Social conditions—Juvenile literature. 3. Depressions—1929—Great Plains—Juvenile literature. 4. Agriculture—Great Plains—History—20th century—Juvenile literature. 5. Droughts—Great Plains—History—20th century—Juvenile literature. 6. Children—Great Plains—History—20th century—Juvenile literature. [1. Dust storms—Great Plains. 2. Great Plains—Social conditions. 3. Depressions—1929. 4. Agriculture—Great Plains—History. 5. Droughts—Great Plains—History.] I. Title. II. Series.
    F595.C78 2000
    978'.032—dc21   98-49041

Manufactured in the United States of America
1 2 3 4 5 6 – JR – 05 04 03 02 01 00

CONTENTS

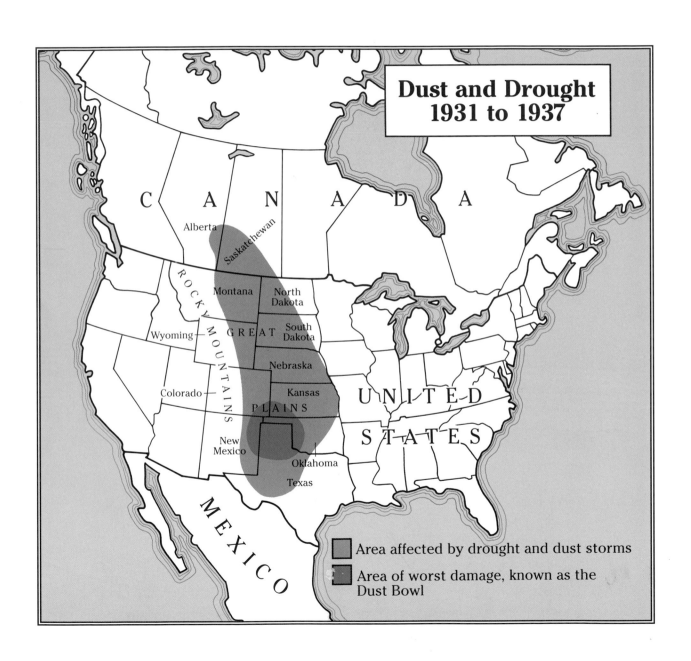

**Dust and Drought
1931 to 1937**

CANADA

Alberta
Saskatchewan

ROCKY MOUNTAINS

Montana

North
Dakota

Wyoming

GREAT

South
Dakota

PLAINS

Nebraska

Colorado

Kansas

UNITED

New
Mexico

STATES

Oklahoma

Texas

MEXICO

Area affected by drought and dust storms

Area of worst damage, known as the
Dust Bowl

Black Blizzards

Rain quit and the wind got high,
And a black old dust storm filled the sky . . .[©]
—words to "Talking Dust Bowl,"
a song by Woody Guthrie

No rain! Year after year, no rain! Ponds dried up. Soil cracked. Drought gripped the plains of North America. Between 1931 and 1937, the dry land spread from Texas to the prairies of Canada. Life there became hard for children and their parents.

When a bit of rain fell, crops sprouted. Then grasshoppers came. They munched the new plants down to the ground. Sometimes the 'hoppers even ate the wash drying on the line.

North Dakota. Grasshoppers dashed the hopes of the family that planted this corn.

Alberta, Canada. A dark dust storm approaches the town of Pearce.

With no rain, few seeds sprouted. No roots grew to hold the earth in place. Wind lifted the soil from the dry, plowed fields. The wind flung the soil across the land. Billowing dust clouds looked like black blizzards. The soil sometimes blew all the way to the Atlantic Ocean. It drifted down on ships at sea.

Oklahoma. Like people, animals needed protection from the dust.

People could see the dust clouds coming. Town children quickly gathered their marbles and balls and headed home. Farm children helped herd animals into the barn.

New Mexico. A girl washes her hands in a bowl of precious water.

Water was scarce during the drought. After washing hands and faces, people saved the water to scrub clothes. Only then did they use it to clean floors.

Oklahoma. Fences had to be raised so they wouldn't be buried by the dust.

On farms, children helped dig out buried equipment. They rescued half-buried chickens and pigs. They cleaned gritty dust out of cows' nostrils.

Fence posts needed to be raised. Then the next storm wouldn't bury the fences and make them useless. Children tried not to touch metal while working. Right after a storm, static electricity filled the air. ZAP! Metal gave a strong shock.

After chores, children had fun searching for arrowheads. They were easier to find with the topsoil scoured away.

South Dakota. Dust piles up on a farm, covering buildings and fences.

Year after year, the dust flew. Even when no wind blew, fine dust hung in the air, sifting down like dirty flour. The plains of North America had become a huge field of dust. One area was even drier and dustier than the rest. People called that area the Dust Bowl. The dust buried towns, farms, wagons, trucks, and animals. It buried people's hopes and dreams.

Left: A family dressed in feed sacks and rags
Opposite page: Farm equipment was useless when crops wouldn't grow.

Dreams Turn to Dust

*If you would like to have your heart broken,
just come out here. This is the dust-storm country.
It is the saddest land I have ever seen.*
—written by Ernie Pyle,
a journalist, in 1936

With no grass to eat, animals starved to death. With no cows to milk and no gardens to harvest, families grew hungry. They ate jackrabbits, even prickly thistles.

Farmers had no crops to sell, so they had no money to buy clothes. Children stuffed cardboard into their worn shoes or went barefoot. In cold weather, they wrapped empty flour or feed sacks around their feet. They even wore dresses and underwear made from these scratchy sacks.

Families couldn't afford gas for their cars. Some took out the engine. They hitched horses to the front.

Most families stayed put during those tough times. But with no money to pay bills, many people lost their businesses, houses, or farms. Some found new homes nearby and tried to start over.

Saskatchewan, Canada. In the 1930s, when Canadians took out car engines and hitched the cars to animals—usually horses—they called the contraptions Bennett Buggies, after Prime Minister R. B. Bennett.

Oklahoma. A family packs furniture for a trip to a new home.

    Others wanted to get away from the dust. Grown-ups wanted jobs and new homes. They wanted fresh air and healthy food for their children. Many of the children had never been more than a few miles from home. Leaving friends and relatives behind made them sad. But the adventure ahead seemed exciting— and scary.

Alberta, Canada. Members of this Canadian family squeezed everything they owned—including their cows—into their wagon when they moved.

Canadians from the prairies moved west to British Columbia, east to Ontario, or even across the ocean to Great Britain. Canada's wheat land lost one quarter of its population.

Oklahoma. On the way to California in 1936

In the United States, about 2.5 million people left their homes in the South and the Great Plains. Some people went to Idaho, Oregon, and Washington.

Others had heard that farms in California needed workers to pick fruits and vegetables. Between 1935 and 1940, over one million people headed west to California.

Oklahoma. This family walks a long road in search of a better life.

Some families hitchhiked to their new homes. They carried a few belongings in battered suitcases. Others walked—day after day, week after week—pushing wheelbarrows or pulling handcarts.

A jalopy sits piled high with pots, a broom, and a table.

Families jammed their belongings into wagons or beat-up trucks and cars called jalopies. They shoved in mattresses—sometimes even a goat. Often the load towered high above their heads.

Children sometimes perched on top of the wobbly load. Then the stuffed vehicle chugged away from the abandoned home and down the road. The children checked ropes to make sure the load didn't come loose.

Days were long, but there were many new sights for a game of I Spy.

Oklahoma. Girls travel with the furniture in the back of their family's jalopy.

California. Washing up in a desert spring

Families ate and slept along the road. They washed their dishes, their clothing, and themselves in streams and ditches. Food was hard to find. With luck, families had boiled potatoes or carrots for dinner. Sometimes carrot tops, apple cores, or coffee grounds were all children had to eat.

Oklahoma. It's dinnertime for a family on the move.

A map made a good tablecloth. A family could eat and plan the next day's journey at the same time. Then, the weary children would snuggle down next to the campfire and sleep.

California. A family enjoys supper in a government-rented cabin in 1939.

At last the United States government helped. In California, it built new camps. For one dollar a week, a family got a one-room tin cabin or a tent built on a wooden platform. The children had toilets to flush, and hot showers. A penny bought breakfast.

Arizona. Playing jacks was one way to have fun.

   At the camp playgrounds, children played tag, mumblety-peg, and baseball. They read comic books, entered wrestling and boxing matches, and went to dances on Saturday night. Buses picked them up to go to Sunday School.

California. School brought new challenges for children from the Dust Bowl.

The children could attend the local school. But school life wasn't always pleasant. While traveling, boys and girls had fallen behind in their learning. Local children called them "dumb Okies" or worse names. They teased them about their clothes. Some teachers thought the children couldn't learn. They "nag and look at you like a dirty dish rag," wrote twelve-year-old Myrle.

California. These children were among the first students at Weedpatch School, a school built by and for children of migrant families near Bakersfield. Weedpatch School had its own crops and livestock, a swimming pool, and an airplane the students used to learn mechanics.

Some of the families gave up and headed back to the dusty plains. But many stayed. They worked when they could. The children went to school and learned. Slowly they became part of the community.

Two young survivors of the dust

The children of the dust days had traveled thousands of dreary miles to find a new life. They had lived through the black blizzards. They had been hungry and poor. But they had survived the drought and dust. And that had made them strong.

AFTERWORD

The wind has always blown across the American plains. Droughts have always come and gone. But for centuries, the roots of prairie grasses held the soil tightly. Then farmers plowed up millions of acres of grasses and planted wheat. Livestock was crowded onto what grassland was left. The animals chewed down the grass and pawed up the roots. In the early 1930s, the rain stopped and the farmers' wheat died. With no grass roots or wheat roots to hold it, soil flew with the wind.

Years later, when rain came at last, people who had stayed on their farms planted new crops. Some who had left the Dust Bowl returned to farms and began again.

Modern farmers use new methods to protect soil and save moisture. They plant many different crops, often in narrow strips. They plow in ways that trap rainfall and prevent soil from blowing. They plant trees to shelter the land.

People cannot make the rain fall or halt the wind. But we can keep the wind from carrying away the soil. The sad times of the dust days need not come again.

DUST DAYS CLOTHING
How to Make a Burlap Shirt

Fall is school and new books, sometimes new shoes and new clothes out of the Montgomery Ward Catalog, but not always, sometimes just homemade feed sack dresses and last year's shoes.
— Roxanne Dunbar-Ortiz,
who grew up during the dust days

People often didn't have enough money for new clothes during the days of the dust storms. Back then, flour was packaged in cotton sacks. Crop seeds and feed for animals came in large sacks made from burlap, a rough, scratchy, brown fabric. When the sacks were empty, mothers washed them and used them to make clothes. The sacks did not make very stylish clothing, but it was better than nothing at all.

Modern flour, animal feed, and crop seeds commonly come in paper bags, but if empty cloth sacks are available, you can easily turn them into shirts. Simply cut holes for the head and arms. If cloth sacks aren't available, burlap can be found at most fabric, craft, and gardening stores.

Burlap Shirt

flexible tape measure
½ yard burlap (approximate) per child*
black magic marker
scissors
2 safety pins
yarn
large-eyed, blunt-end needle

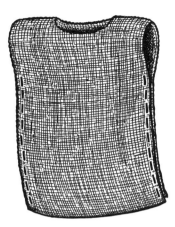

1. Using a flexible tape measure, measure the distance from the tip of one shoulder to the tip of your other shoulder. Spread the rectangle of burlap flat, so a long edge is facing you. Place the tape measure on top of the fabric, starting at one edge. Use a magic marker to mark off the span of your shoulders. Repeat, marking in the middle and at the other edge.

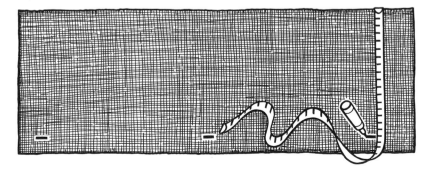

* Widths for burlap vary, but you should have a rectangle of cloth.

42

2. Use a scissors to cut in a straight line from one marking to the next, removing the excess fabric.

3. Fold the short ends of fabric together. To make a neck opening, make a small snip with the scissors in the center of the fold. Then enlarge the snip, cutting from the center along the fold approximately 4 inches in either direction.

4. For armholes, measure 6 inches below the fold on each side. Secure the fabric below each armhole with a safety pin.

5. Measure 3 feet of yarn. Thread the yarn through a large-eyed, blunt-end needle. Knot the yarn end. Sew one side seam of the shirt, starting at the bottom of one armhole and ending at the bottom edge of the shirt. Keep your sewing to within ½ to 1 inch of the fabric edge. Knot the end of the yarn. Repeat your sewing on the opposite edge. Remove the safety pins. Turn your shirt inside out if desired.

6. Wear the shirt next to your skin for as long as you can stand it.

NOTE TO TEACHERS AND ADULTS

For children, the dust days may seem like part of a far-off past. But there are many ways to make this era and its people come alive. Along with helping children learn to make burlap shirts, you can explore America's Dust Bowl past in other ways. One way is to read more about the era. More books on the topic are listed on page 46. Another way to explore the past is to train young readers to study historical photographs. Historical photographs hold many clues about how life was lived in earlier times.

Ask your children or students to look for the details and "read" all the information in each picture in this book. For example, how many children in Dust Bowl photographs are wearing shoes?

To encourage young readers to learn to read historical photographs, have them try these activities:

On the Road

Look at the photographs of families on the road on pages 20 through 29. When forced to leave their homes in the Dust Bowl, what kinds of things did families take with them? On a piece of paper in one column, under the heading "dust days," list the items you can see in the photographs. Next, set aside time in the evening or on a weekend to interview your parents or another older person who had to move as a child. What items did they take along? List those items on paper under the heading "my parents' day." Finally, in a third column, under the heading "my day," list the items you would take if you had to leave your home and move across the country. How do the lists differ? How are they the same? What would you take if—like children in the dust days—you could pack only one cardboard box?

Writing Letters

From the point of view, or perspective, of one of the children shown in this book, write a letter about your life. If you choose to write from the point of view of a child in the drought area, write a letter to a friend whose family has moved west in search of work. Or put yourself in the place of a child shown on the road west and write a letter to a friend who has stayed in the Dust Bowl. Or write a letter from the point of view of a child in a migrant worker camp. How has your life changed because of the drought? If you are on the road, what do you expect to find at the end of your travels? If you are already in the west, what do you miss most? What's the best thing about your new life?

Who Helps Those in Need?

The photographs on pages 35 through 38 show children and their families living in camps for migrant workers. The government created these camps to help people who had to leave their homes in the Dust Bowl. In modern times, victims of natural disasters can turn to many sources for help. Choose a recent American drought, flood, earthquake, hurricane, tornado, or wildfire. Then look for stories about that disaster in magazines, newspapers, or on the Internet. After you have looked at stories and photos, list the groups—from government agencies to volunteers to nonprofit organizations—who help those in need.

Resources on the Dust Days

Andryszewski, Tricia. *Dust Bowl: Disaster on the Plains.* Brookfield, Conn.: The Millbrook Press, 1993. Andryszewski describes how nature and people combined to create the Dust Bowl and what we can do to prevent another devastating drought.

Hesse, Karen. *Out of the Dust.* New York: Scholastic Press, 1997. This Newbery Award–winning book, written in free verse, tells the story of fourteen-year-old Billie Jo, who faces tragedy on her family's dusty Oklahoma wheat farm.

Porter, Tracey. *Treasures in the Dust.* New York: Joanna Cotler Books, an imprint of HarperCollins Publishers, 1997. Through the stories of two friends, Annie and Violet, Porter's novel paints a picture of the harshness and the beauty of life in Cimarron County, Oklahoma, in the 1930s.

Raven, Margot Theis. Illustrated by Roger Essley. *Angels in the Dust.* Mahwah, N.J.: BridgeWater Books, 1997. In this picture book, Great-grandma Annie remembers her growing-up years in Oklahoma in the 1930s.

Stanley, Jerry. *Children of the Dust Bowl: The True Story of the School at Weedpatch Camp.* New York: Crown Publishers, Inc., 1992. Historian Stanley tells the story of a school built by and for the children of dust days migrants in California.

Website   http://www.pbs.org/wgbh/pages/amex/dustbowl/
This site was designed to provide more information to viewers of the PBS television program "Surviving the Dust Bowl," part of the American Experience series.

New Words

blizzard: usually a bad snowstorm with strong winds. During the dust days, bad dust storms were sometimes called "black blizzards."

cheesecloth: a light, loosely woven cotton fabric

drought: a long period of dry weather. During the dust days, the period of dry weather lasted from about 1931 through 1937.

Dust Bowl: the area in Kansas, Colorado, New Mexico, Texas, and Oklahoma that suffered most from the dust storms of the 1930s

lard: cooking grease made from pig fat

mumblety-peg: a children's game played with a pocketknife. The knife has to be flipped in certain ways so that it sticks into the dirt.

Okie: the name given to people who migrated to California from the drought lands. At first, it meant a person from Oklahoma. Later, after many migrants arrived in California, it came to mean a person who was not welcome or acceptable.

relief: financial help from the government given to those in need

Index

TIME LINE

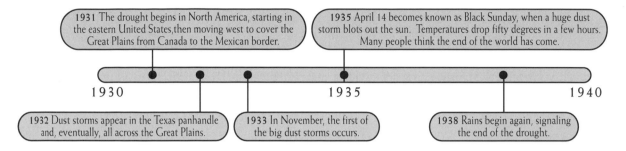

1931 The drought begins in North America, starting in the eastern United States, then moving west to cover the Great Plains from Canada to the Mexican border.

1935 April 14 becomes known as Black Sunday, when a huge dust storm blots out the sun. Temperatures drop fifty degrees in a few hours. Many people think the end of the world has come.

1930   1935   1940

1932 Dust storms appear in the Texas panhandle and, eventually, all across the Great Plains.

1933 In November, the first of the big dust storms occurs.

1938 Rains begin again, signaling the end of the drought.

ABOUT THE AUTHOR

Karen Mueller Coombs grew up in the northern Alberta, Canada, town of Grande Prairie. In the 1930s, the dust reached even that far north, she says. Her mother recalls children wearing underwear made from flour sacks and re-members coming home from school to find layers of dust on the windowsills.

A former elementary school teacher, Karen lives with her family in Carlsbad, California. "As a child, I lived in the country," she says. "I re-member dust getting in my eyes whenever the wind blew and coming home from windy track meets with my scalp covered with dirt. But I can't imagine living through a black blizzard. Not being able to take a deep breath because the air was thick with dust must have been a terrifying feeling."

ACKNOWLEDGMENTS

The author wishes to thank Robert Allen Rutland, Wilma Elizabeth McDaniel, and Roxanne Dunbar-Ortiz for sharing their memories of the dust days; and her writing group, for their encouragement and wisdom. The publisher gratefully acknowledges the use of quotations from the following sources: Roxanne Dunbar-Ortiz, *Red Dirt: Growing Up Okie*. New York: Verso, 1997; Ann Marie Low, *Dust Bowl Diary*. Lincoln, Neb.: University of Nebraska Press, 1984; T. H. Watkins, *The Great Depression*. New York: Little, Brown and Company, 1993; "Talking Dust Bowl," ("Talking Dust Blues"), words and music by Woody Guthrie, TRO© Copyright 1960 (Renewed) 1963 (Renewed) Ludlow Music Inc., New York, New York. Used by Permission. The photographs in this book are reproduced through the courtesy of: Library of Congress, front and back covers (LC-USF34-004047-E and LC-USF34-004627-E), pp. 1 (LC-USF33-003646-M2), 2 (LC-USF34-004635-D), 5 (LC-USF34-2506-E), 7 (LC-USF34-4053-E), 8 (LC-USF34-21049-C), 10 (LC-USF34-004048-E), 11 (LC-USZ62-11491), 13 (LC-USZ62-35798), 14 (LC-USF34-33470-D), 15 (LC-USF33-12739-M4), 16 (LC-USF34-004051-E), 18 (LC-USF33-000553-M4), 19 (LC-USF33-12552-M3), 21 (LC-USF33-12316-M2), 23 (LC-USF33-2372-M3), 25 (LC-USF34-19360-E), 26 (LC-USF33-12312-M1), 27 (LC-USF34-T01-16451-C), 28 (LC-USF33-12276-M5), 29 (LC-USF34-18191-E), 30 (LC-USF34-4871-D), 31 (LC-USF34-21049-C), 33 (LC-USF34-T01-16269-C), 34 (LC-USF34-9995C), 36 (LC-USF33-012681-M2), 37 (LC-USF34-16106-C), 39 (LC-USF34-2978-E), 40 (LC-USF34-18262-C); Laura Westlund, pp. 6, 42; Glenbow Archives, Calgary, Canada, pp. 9 (NA-1831-1), 22 (ND-3-6343); Schomburg Center/The New York Public Library/Astor, Lenox, and Tilden Foundations, p. 12; National Archives, p. 17 (114-DL-SD-5000); Saskatchewan Archives Board, p. 20 (R-A 19,945); Corbis-Bettmann, p. 24; UPI/Corbis-Bettmann, pp. 32, 35; Jerry Stanley, from *Children of the Dust Bowl: The True Story of the School at Weedpatch Camp*, p. 38.